Hide & Seek

Shadow Poetry

by Helen Condon Powell

....

"Time flies over us but leaves its
shadow behind."

Nathaniel Hawthorne

PALMETTO
PUBLISHING
Charleston, SC
www.PalmettoPublishing.com

Hide & Seek
Copyright © 2023 by Helen Condon Powell

First Edition

Hardcover ISBN: 979-8-8229-1752-1
Paperback ISBN: 979-8-8229-1753-8

Among Many, Special Thanks to

Andrey Gergel
Beatrice Espovich
Bill Condon
Constantine Manos
Dan Smith
Edith Heyck
Eric Condon
Gerhard Eichler
Graham Bell
Hector Martinez
Jean Lightman
Jerry Cosgrove
John Unni

Julian Buxton
Kelly Easton
Kristi Condon
Lisette Model
Lucy Wilhelm
Margaret Mahoney
Marie Harris
Mimi Baird
Minor White
Raphaela Platow
Swift Barnes
Thea Fournier

All Photographs & Paintings by
Helen C. Powell

Table of Contents

RESILIENCE

HOPES & DREAMS

RELATIONSHIPS

"Art enables us to find ourselves and
lose ourselves at the same time."

Thomas Merton

Give & Take

Unsure, even in my pretty dress
I try to rebalance after a fast turn,
then decide to pause.

But the rhythm won't wait
and I am drawn into the future
even as memories pull me back.

I unstrap my dance shoes
undo the fancy white hair
replace one of many masks
and take a cup of Covid Acceptance
in this Pandemic Twilight Zone.

Some will survive better than others
choosing past over present to
Make America Great Again.
Others worry that global warming
will finally fix our mistakes.

I pull into the driveway of friends
as they downsize and leave
just as I downsize, stay behind
and wonder about the push and pull.
The give and take. The then and now.

Time Warp

Memory is the author of future stories
that reshape feelings about the past
so we can live in the present
and create new memories
about tomorrow.

The Other Life

The clown gently embraces his partner
guiding her around the dance floor.
His enormous top hat and satin tuxedo
matches her checkered costume
while his red nose nods with the beat.

Holiday guests sip champagne
in bemused admiration
wondering who they are.
Some glance at the program card.
Others simply chuckle.

They wiggle their jolly waltz--
a career escape for him
and kitchen escape for her--
as their choreographer on the sidelines
smiles at them both and his own
life-detour talents.

Two Bracelets

Might my graduating niece
prefer a gold bangle bracelet
to my weekend plane ticket?
Should I get a second gold treat
closer to me in age and price?

In this old plantation city
a few little diamonds would surely
flatter my solitary-stamina age.
And she would still have the bangle.

The bangle was dutifully engraved
while the saleslady secured
my chain's discreet little clasp
until I took off my sweater in the heat.

When the safety catch failed
I searched the summer shade-tree grass
only to realize my brief little bracelet
was just another family mystery
I'd keep to myself.

Scorecard Friends

One slices into the woods
while another hopes her caution
will earn a par or even a birdie.
Walking across the fairway
I see deer watching from the trees.

A lucky ball emerges from the woods
while a chip shot falls short
and it's my turn to try for the green.
I wonder about the pond, the sand
and some impervious geese.

Sometimes I'm carefree in the fresh air,
other times prayerfully uncertain
about the indoor virus and global warming
that bring us safely outdoors
for our weekly, dimpled-ball dialogue.

Ups & Downs

When are friends there
but not there?

Writing instead of calling
Calling instead of writing
Seeing but not hearing
Hearing but not seeing?

Do they lift us up
or just let us down?

Ships Passing

Should I linger
just a moment?
Pause to exchange
a little wisdom
along the way?
Or let them hurry on
to a meditation class
about The Power of Now?

Food for Thought

Not quite in the moment
we invent the past, fear the future
and focus on guest arrivals
their room assignments
and pillow preferences.

When did we start to orchestrate
houseguest happiness
then bow to decorator dictums
and dance to food guru tunes?
Julia Child could say something pithy
about the absurdity of it all.

Oatmeal cookies once soothed us
after midday fishing on the dock.
But now, food philosophy is
a litany of allergy fears.
Should we eschew the rack of lamb
lured from another continent?

Between curves and cravings
portions and waistlines
we shift between spinach and spandex
tiny tops and big bottoms
big tops and tight bottoms.

Some guests bring their presence
While others bring ripe cheese
and leave after three days
as a nod to Miss Manners.

Garden Mystery

Fifty years later
I still stand that way
hands folded,
right hand on top of left.

How did I know
standing in that garden,
to be so still?
So calm . . .

I didn't feel very calm at the time.
He was the visionary
and I the student.
Would I be smart enough
to say the right things?

I waited for some warmth
to come up from the soil
and remind him, clever though he was,
that I was beside him.

But he didn't move.

His handsome beard
and evasive pipe smoke
told me his admiring students
already had more of him than I.

Thirteen years to the day
we parted in a judge's cold chamber
as if that hopeful garden moment
had never even happened.

Past Glory

The ghosts of this Charleston mansion
are not quite gone.

I look at the marble sink:
a forgotten fixture is suspended from the wall
with no faucet, drain or water connect.

All is gone from the house, except for this sink
and a harp in the next room.

I imagine the conscience of uneasy ancestors
coming into town on Sundays
to escape rice-field heat and malaria.

Did someone play the harp to forget?
Or to remember?

The guide sticks to his script.
The house can no longer
answer questions, or speak for itself.

Only a lingering ghost or two
visits the marble sink
or plays the abandoned harp
after the day's last visitor is gone
and the ghosts are put to rest.

Family Album

Sophia, Claire and Gabriella
smile for the camera in muted gray satin.
Their sashes and bows
hardly move in a soft Texas breeze.

A visit to their orderly home
its tidy living room décor
and sleek kitchen counters
complete the picture.

I search for details that might provide clues.
Hair color, bone structure, jewelry or posture.
Who are these careful young women
and what will become of them?

I look at the wedding occasion photo
and focus on two more.
Flaxen-haired Maya is posed
squarely in front of the others.

She gazes with such a measured
Nordic smile that I wonder
whether she knows I am watching.
What is in the back of her mind?

Then I see raven-haired Monika,
whose cheerful smile assures me
and her Latino grandmother nearby
there's room for us all
in the Family Album.

Condo Assessment

On rainy nights
roof water would trickle silently
behind condo stucco
on to our patios
and into our living rooms.

Crumbling stucco fell five floors.
Leaky windows went to the dumpster.
Patio drains failed to cope.
Insurance policies struggled,
as we faced a lawsuit-shortfall.

Should we sell?
Or weather the weather?

Each morning the foreman listened
to the dialects of nimble bricklayers.
By noon the taco truck was abuzz
while we ate our quiche and wished
we cared less about calories.

At precisely four, chattering trucks
poured out of the garage gate
and the building went quiet until morning
When repairs resumed
to our wistful condos by the sea.

Ancestral Cottage

Wattle was used with lattice, he said,
on colonial walls daubed with straw.
It broke down over time
revealing the rustic stamina
of New England settler family cottages.

Milky-glass windows and bend-low doorways
now welcome the cottage descendants
as sunlight through a window
falls upon a slept flat pillow.
Wide floorboards support footsteps
that echo those of our ancestors.

The guide has studied colonial history
since his circus youth when
juggling and twirling cane skills
slowly swirled into stories
of local farm and coastal sea mastery.
He is more nimble than any of us.

Setting his silver-trimmed cane aside
and pausing to see our reactions
he conceals his own remarkable story
as he tells visitors what life was like
before Ancestry.com and indoor plumbing.

Party Styles

For some
a baby shower,
class reunion or office party
are ways to improve
mingling skills.

For others
mingling sidelines
become social snapshots
from the Album of Neglect.

While still others simply swirl
around the room looking
looking for pretty nibbles on a tray.

The Music Lesson

My talented mother leans forward
and gazes dreamily over her little elbow
as she imagines singing in Carnegie Hall.
My runaway grandmother
who had escaped a timber tycoon father
and married a Quiet Southerner
plays the piano with graceful assurance.
My aunt stands dutifully behind
little suspecting she will be held for ransom
by a disgruntled employee of her husband.

The soft-focus scene suggests
a waltz in satin and lace.
A polished floor reflects a mahogany chair,
a white dress and a chandelier
for this rising Kentucky family.
Barely visible, gilded frames suggest
landscapes before the Great Depression.
Their future is yet to unfold
as their graceful figures and folds
seem timeless in their legacy moment.

Family fortunes were lost and then found.
My aunt's kidnapping evolved into
a love of gardens and a watchful eye
on the next generation or two.
My mother gave up her musical dreams
falling under the spell of suburban security.

She kept these thoughts to herself
as she gently reminded her children
and far-off grandchildren
Life is not always what it seems.

Free Wi-Fi

The café was filled with long empty cups.
Students were plugged into laptop power,
enjoying the tuition-paid cliques,
without any dorm-access worries.

When I rhetorically asked
How long have you been here?
they decided to look blank then
checked email and gazed out the window.

Wanting only a little coffee
and a bite to eat with a friend
I stood resolutely in a sea
of wifi tables and chairs.

When I again queried,
a student waiting only for soup
looked resigned to the reality
of coffee cup power.

She mentioned sitting
on hallway floors
while others lived in the dorms.
She tried not to cry.

With full-tuition composure
the empty cups listened to her story
about the daily commute
from her parents' house.

When her soup-story voice went quiet
I could only ponder the logic of
tuition money and dorm life
unfairness of it.

Rain Refuge

A solid wall of water
tumbling from the roof
woke me from a deep sleep.
Ground cover could not muffle
the sound of a coastal storm.

I walked in night-gowned darkness
out the living room door
heard the slap and splash
of the season's tropical storm
echoing off the patio walls
then whirling the rainwater away.

Outlined against the sky
iridescent lighting, a pause
and a boom a few seconds up the coast
helped me track the storm before
another jagged bolt,
and another even louder boom.

I remember another downpour. . . .

With shampoo and comb
I stood under a big elm
my tiny feet sinking
into a cushion of warm grass.
I showered unnoticed
in a summer rain.

I looked back at the house
whose silent antiques
and manicured lawns
could not soothe
my anxious mother
or the moody-needy sister.

Combing my tangled hair
I wrapped a thick towel
around my shivering shoulders
and quietly acknowledged
the mysteries of families
and uncertain weather.

Cinderella

Running soapy water through my fingers
I realized that the oil wells had
financed powder room bouquets
that were much nicer than grocery store choices.

Wincing at my reflection in the mirror,
I decided to remember the good years
and make a wedding obligation
into a witness occasion.

The once fit father of the groom
looked at the youth-filled dance floor
and his own frail son starting out on his own.
I thought about being the outlier aunt
from the liberal Northeast.

What will become of the couple,
The father and the others, for that matter?

A bent and bookish brother
squinted at a wedding ritual
quite beneath his Libertarian politics.
Our portly brother barely nodded in my direction
as he mumbled a joke to his thin new wife.

Carefree granddaughters chatted
under the relaxed gaze of mothers
that our brothers might prefer to ignore.
I remembered our beleaguered mother,
and nearly forgotten regrets.

Wondering who on earth to talk to
I studied the deckle-edged menu
and the surf and turf
so stylishly arranged
on rented plates.

Two restless hours later
my tired witness eyes
returned me to the powder room mirror.
Whereupon a souvenir bouquet escorted me
to my car and a hotel room in the middle of nowhere.

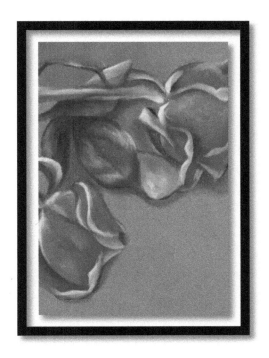

SOLITUDE

"I dwell in possibility."

Emily Dickinson

The Oak Leaf

What could be more relaxing,
the guidebook assured me,
than Thanksgiving weekend
at the Grove Park Inn?

At dusk the mountaintop courtyard
was filled with chaos that made me wonder
about my little holiday, alone
amidst all this family harmony.
My little Ford had lost its Focus
among a forest of valet-driven betters.

I felt invisible at the front desk check-in.
With only a little luggage, I tried to be brave.

The dinner menu failed to enchant me
but a woodland walk gifted an oak leaf
of such bronze perfection
it became my room's windowsill witness.
Should I sketch my leafy companion
or take a little photograph home?

The courtyard below was still busy
with bigger cars and larger tips than mine.
Cranky children and their grandparents
suddenly came into a late-day focus
as I realized that my bedside reading
might be even better than *Saturday Night Live*.

Taupe

My tulip pitcher by the door
invites book club visitors
to imagine watery landscapes
and pulsing windmills.

Three hundred years later,
the flower breeders' mania
has become my still life's
uncertain sign of spring.

Made from palette-wheel opposites
taupe clings to my bristle brushes
while the tulips on my canvas
simply ask for a passing nod.

Care Packages

Brown paper with stars.
Bright colors with bows.
She leaves them, door after door,
hoping friends will know
what to do with her generosity.

A word, an invitation
a compliment, a question
as she waits down the street
to see which doors will open
which packages taken inside.

Sometimes she gives advice
helps when help isn't wanted
notices when she shouldn't
cares when they don't.

Time Passes.
Should she ring some door bells
or just wait for them to notice
she was once there?

Laundry Lines

Looking out the train window
stop-action views made me question
a world without pretty wallpaper,
polo ponies and Dad's advice.

Flashes of simple cotton dresses and
a dark-haired girl about my age
made me wonder about city stress
and suburban ease.

When we went to Tiffany
Dad bought me a gold heart-shaped pin
to remember a tenth birthday.
He warned me there are no free rides
even from the suburbs.

Work hard, he said.
Be curious, grateful,
independent and even stubborn.
In case you have to be.

My mahogany hair is white
as I look out the window and remember
words of caution about trading places
with cotton dresses and unknown lives.

Rain Drops

I returned South after a light rain
and a numbing Yankee summer
sorting through family crises,
one stubborn box at a time.
I needed a staycation.

I would be less worried,
try some new hobbies and start anew!
Maybe my sleep would improve
and my blood pressure return to normal.
Whatever normal was those stormy days.

I grabbed a rain hat and remembered
sitting on a log in the woods
inspecting bugs, worms and butterflies.
Listening to the sound of crows in the meadow
a hidden waterfall and a dirt road beyond.

I prepared the garden soil for winter,
unwound that ball of family yarn
then settled inside with a good book
to resolve mind clutter
one blessed raindrop at a time.

Halloween

Pumpkin-colored drapes
had been tied back to
frame the balcony sign:
John Pope Antiques.

The ecclesiastical word
tickled my funny bone in this city
known for its many churches.

A narrow building had been rented
to someone who needed a special place.
That season, it was a dealer in small things.

Wondering what mystery I might find
I climbed up one flight and found
an open door into total darkness.

I squinted and then inhaled.
Old-knowledge books lined the room
giving off the incense of first editions.

Jewelry in glass cases
sparkled like fireflies
along with pens and letter openers.

An antique birdcage
completed the feeling of Halloween
as I thumbed through a copy of "The Raven."

From behind a torn curtain
a young man with a trim mustache
gestured toward a dusty writing desk
once owned, he murmured,

by Edgar Allan Poe.

Symphony Tales

Worthy donors stroll past
gold-rimmed tables,
endless stemware,
pomegranates and posies.
All in support of symphony salaries.

I join a young couple from the suburbs
whose children will hear about
the cello and the choir
the piano and the soprano
and the food for fussy grownups.

When concert hall lights blink
we drift apart as others air-kiss
their newly found, long-lost friends
and I sit at a gold-rimmed table
with new-money party donors.

To a place card nearby, I murmur
admiration of smoked salmon,
tender beef and frisée salad.
To the one on my left, I say
the mousse is perfect with the Madeira.

As my program slips off my sleepy lap
I envy the children at home
with their cookies and milk
eager for bedtime-story magic
from their gala-evening parents.

One by One

they slowly add up.

One tiny drop of rain
after another quietly
falling on summer leaves
above a silent roof
down to a footpath below
steadily joining forces.

Like tears gathering
after a storm
as I put down the phone
and wonder why people
argue with reality
or even the weather.

Meditation

I put my city garden flowers
on the kitchen counter
and fill the blue vase with water
this late summer afternoon.

Looking out the window
I remember visiting Beacon Hill,
whose townhouses were shuttered
against our photo course curiosity.

Between visits, he sent flowers
to remind me of his rose garden in Tokyo.

But his frail kindness is now gone
as I watch water rush into the vase
and measure and trim the stems,
feeling comforted by it all.

Dahlias, lilies, and irises
scarlet, persimmon, and lavender
slowly become orange, yellow, and violet
in the gently fading light.

Then a small white dove
comes in the window
and alights onto a lone rose
transporting me to Tokyo
in my little Zen moment.

Art Show Annie

Has she been left on a windowsill
by an admirer of art? Or by a lost child?

Her button eyes watch strolling patrons
so very serious and smart
about wine and art.

Just outside the colonial glass window
late-day sunshine softens the mood
of this stalwart shipbuilding town.

Today it's a trendy art scene
where artists and investors chatter
as she whispers:

Please smile back.

Motif #1

Perched on an old stone pier,
this little red barn waits and watches
for summer visitors and lobster boats
to notice its iconic shape.

Hanging buoys silently dot its sides
like sheet music notes
played by festival talent
hoping for critical acclaim.

For a few short months
this endearing symbol
of coastal New England awakens
and whispers to sea symphony lovers,
"Please, capture me on canvas."

Solitude

Sister,

Hang your chair
with its finely woven seat,
upside down on a peg by the window.

Outside cross-rail fencing
still defines well-weeded fields
and serenely grazing sheep.

Your perfectly turned finials
do credit to this cool Kentucky glen
that was once Shaker Town.

Fading Light

I arrive at this hilltop estate
and sit on a gnarled bench
waiting for a guided tour of Olana.

Exotic tiles cover the exterior
while late-day gardeners manicure
the scenery outside his studio windows.

When his Victorian image of nature faded
he accepted his fate, the guard said, and
yet stayed on his mountaintop.

Returning to the gnarled bench
I think of his once-majestic career,
all but forgotten by history.

His landscapes hang on dark parlor walls
as visitors try to grasp their meaning.
They browse the gift shop then go for lunch.

Musing about career highs and lows
I accept my modest ambitions
and decide with no regret
that I am as big for me
as he once was, for him.

The Book Signing

The charming side streets
of this old library city
invite visitors, writers
and some talented chefs
to a literary festival reception.

I set aside my glass of Merlot
to sit and rest my tired feet.
Nearby, a portly man with a red face
and watery eyes gazes at people
who admire his editorial magic.

My brown velvet pants and silk blouse
are as discreet as the quiet poems
languishing in my purse.
Would anyone notice me standing
in the signature-table line?

While a chef puts some shrimp atop the grits
and adds an artful drizzle
writers at the whiskey bar
speculate about agents and publishers
eager, or perhaps reluctant, to discover new talent.

Armchair Travel

Postings on Facebook have replaced
postcards from Afar.
Chicken is grilled not fried.
Wine is white not red.

Recipe cards and cupboard keys
have replaced travel brochures.
I no longer make reservations
or even have them.

The process slows to a crawl
as I downsize to a treasured few:
some old lace, that high school photo
and some leather books.

There's something comforting
about a canvas drop cloth
that folds and unfolds
for this letting-go tableau.

Boxes packed and unpacked,
"Free" signs on the curb,
trips to Goodwill,
bedding to local shelters.

I take the stairs with care
and pass a sea of walking aids
to hear a piano excerpt from *La Mer*
floating in a sea of white hair.

Serene faces hear a familiar melody,
as I follow their gracious lead,
let go of the past and gingerly travel
between lunch and dinner.

Memory Foam

My supportive mattress
knows nothing of my past.
Nor does the mourning dove
outside my window.
I swing my legs floor-ward
and shuffle kitchen-ward.

As my mattress slowly recovers
I hear the toaster jump and I stretch.
I tie my very sensible shoelaces
for a digestive morning walk
toward my revised fitness goals.

The memory of my gracious past
fades over some nostalgic tea
while a little marmalade tells me
to enjoy the new mattress,
my reading chair's view
and kindness of this little moment.

Morning Door Nod

Some people use big gestures
to tell people they are alive.

At my cozy little retirement village
opening my apartment door before noon

tells the nice folks at the front desk
I'm alive and good to go.

Name Game

She struggles with names
and I remind her
names are just an abstraction.
Memory a convenience.
Or a burden.

Mary may not be merry.
Ernst earnest.
Frank frank
Peter patriotic
or William willing.

Just the other day
she smiled her hallway greeting,
paused and again asked,
"Do I know You?"
I said, Yes.
My name is . . . Eugenia.

RESILIENCE

**"What stands in the way
Becomes the way."**

Marcus Aurelius

Resilience

You admit things could be worse
and that you are grateful for
a bit more time.
Then the anger returns.

The hand so essential to daily tasks
no longer cooperates with the other
to push, pull, grasp, let go
or even pound a fist on the table.

Now mute, it considers your past
the parents who did not understand
or who knew you only too well
and the years you tried to win approval
for your business legacy plans.

Morning coffee in the Texas sun
is a new and deliberate ritual.
Despite the appealing décor
and dining room camaraderie
you feel betrayed.

Your mind is sharper than ever,
but you still worry and still obsess.
Therapy trips have redefined your social life
while soft music and easy games
try to shift you into The Power of Now.

Then your patient nurse stops by to say
some also-ailing friends are waiting in the sun
as they remember the good times
and joke about football and politics.

At dinnertime family members
stop by to enjoy your company,
share insights and once again admire
your proud resilience.

Vague Regrets

I suppose we all do it. We seek
then hide in a room full of people
not knowing why we're there
wanting to leave as soon as we arrive.

Our book group sits at a trendy southern bar
discussing tastes in music and food.
Two young chefs flourish flaming pans
while I wonder while someone there
might also be a budding author?

Waiters balance plates of virtuoso food
to the sound of cocktail shaker chatter while
romantic tables-for-two make me wince.
Should I order a Sweet Sidecar
or some Luck of the Irish?

As two musicians arrive with their violin cases
I try not to envy their well-earned fatigue
after a concerto that left us enthralled
in the donor-built concert hall.

Ancient oak trees and their wistful moss
make me question with a twinge.
Why I didn't practice my music longer
start writing poetry sooner
or take that Other Road?

Dear Colon,

This morning's lemon tea
hopes to move you to a fate
my family has little understood.

My father's comfort food
and my brother's detox diet
have offered mixed-message advice,

as I move from the past
to digestive enlightenment
and the light of a porcelain day.

Is it possible that a good night's sleep
is the light at the end of this tunnel?
Will it resolve the un-dissolvable?

Will the indiscrete burger
the indulgent chocolate
and the merry mac 'n' cheese

applaud my recklessness
while I suppress a flatulent murmur
of apology from,

Your Fiber Smart,
Neighbor

High Heels & Low

Chandelier earrings dangle
and long lashes flutter
while I can only look down
at my too-sensible shoes.

When we return from the dance floor
she rocks a high-heel shoe
under my unpowdered nose
while I ask about her spray tan glow.

She has danced her sexy routine
for two expensive years
while my clip-on rhinestones
simply wink at the judges.

You Say Tomato

When we met at the door
you produced subscription tickets
from a designer coat pocket
whose label I hardly knew.

With a vintage purse on my lap
I glanced at the music lovers below
and wondered which came first
your divorce or mine.

Studying the program book
for facts you knew full well
I overheard you mention a man
I knew would never leave his wife.

At intermission your travel plans,
grand opera tickets and
donor-list connections
upstaged my midlife musings.

When I praised the soloist's talent
at a piano that neither of us played
you corrected my naïve enthusiasm
and I thought to myself . . . to-mah-to.

Then you flaunted your black Armani
during the final applause
and I buttoned up my little red wool,
thinking about a Liszt of my own.

The Linen Closet

Once pretty and popular
with chestnut hair, athletic figure
and a knack for languages,
her ghostly memory glides
down the stairs, out the front door
to a lawn once lit by family drama.

She had the boyfriends
while I had the books.
She said I was the weak one
while she was stronger than our mother
sitting by the living room window
coffee in the morning, a cocktail by four.

I remember hiding my confusion
in the linen closet watching a tiny moth
crawl up the wall while flashlight shadows
made soothing images that I sketched
unnoticed, while she made demands
of our two beleaguered parents.

When her teenage skin showed its anxiety
my sister plucked her eyebrows bare.
Childish chatter turned to blame as her
postpartum threats claimed
we knew what was wrong.
We never did.

Many years later I strolled a lawn
that was once such a mystery
and casually mentioned my memoirs
to the new owners of a house
that had once welcomed
my sister's gentlemen callers.

Accidents Happen

A paper cut,
slipping on black ice
a cracked tooth . . .

Speaking in haste,
a bounced check
missing a birthday . . .

Remember to forgive,
practice kindness
and be grateful.

Then embrace
all the close calls
we call Life.

Arch Support

Just when I thought my feet were happy,
my new shoes started squeaking.
The handsome young podiatrist
suggested I try some foot-angel cream.

I worry that my feet might no longer
respond to his flirty caress.
Should I buy Pradas in purple
or Mephistos in mauve?

My mother's feet also struggled.
In footwear confusion,
she decided to ignore the reality
of life's ups and downs.

Shoes are a fact of life, I say.
I put up my feet and accept
the irony of my aging years.
Then I try one more thing.

Baby powder, a friend suggests,
might fix my squeaky shoes
and fallen arches to becalm
my once-flirty feet.

Radiator Shoes

He puts on blue Tyvek booties
as I listen to radiator theories
about big-boiler heating systems.

He's a steam-heat engineer
in a Yankee town where ancient skills
proudly compete with Internet advice.

He replaces a coughing radiator valve
and tweaks piping to another
so that steam can no longer get stuck,
condense and explode inside.

(In the dead of winter
the reassuring hissing of steam
can build up to household thunder.)

Replace the wall thermostat, he says.
Modify the ceiling heater in the bathroom.
Adjust the pipe pitch in the cellar.
That'll prevent those steam-heat noises.

He's kind and convincing.
I hope for the best but am only
cautiously optimistic.

As he takes off his booties
and writes up my bill,
I look down at my New Balance sneakers
and think of shoe alternatives.

FitFlops for seashore strolls,
Mephistos for library days or
Capezios for dance lessons.

Each to extend my health
and my foot ware acceptance
of ancient heating systems.

À La Carte

The food here could be better.
A test of priorities and palates
someone mumbles.

Whether to eat well or live longer.
Gain weight or gain insight.
To digest, digress or divulge
between Bridge, Billiards or Bingo.

Broadway musicals
and banana pudding
have replaced Bizet's *Carmen*
and petits fours.

The waiter's ebony skin
and menu choices are lost
amid the four-score table chatter
of couples bent under the weight

of their Mayflower history
which suddenly seems irrelevant.

Only the first names
for some and the last for others
clarify who's who
in this twilight place.

Two-Ply Issue

Who would have thought
hoarding a virtue
as we scurry out the door
past masked strangers
who were once our friends?

Hiding our smile-less faces
we control this pandemic
by stocking up on toilet paper
in case the beans and rice exhale
and decide to fight back.

Amazing Grace

I inhale the salty sea air,
lift the latch and walk through
the handwrought gate.

Two hundred years ago
the same church bell tolled
in this toiling plantation city
while a trading ship captain
composed his repentant Grace.

Letting Go

The real estate listing describes
a Charming New England Federal
with curb appeal and history.

Up early each morning,
I had sketched boutique-worthy dresses
while he read late into the night.

His boarding school childhood
was followed by career regrets
then clouded by science-fiction paperbacks.

With Yankee discretion
my friends worried about my cheerful energy
and his gloomy retreat.

Moving from room to room
the downsizing and my feelings
now take on lives of their own.

I resist the sentimental twinge,
then call an antiques dealer,
and let the process progress.

Only a few questions remain.
Why did he hide in his books,
then wordlessly depart
that Charming Federal on High Street?

The Vigil

She sips cafeteria coffee,
watches the oxygen monitor
and listens to blood pressure beeps.
He ignores post-op instructions
and insists he'll soon be on his feet,
clocking steps and calling the shots.

Even in his youth
the club champion
and wannabe tycoon
said he was too busy
for paperwork or Trivial Pursuit.

A nurse returns with two pills
another with leg exercise weights
and he goes through the motions.

In a corner of the room
his sister looks at his bruised leg,
reads a bit of *Lost Horizon*
and gently hands him
a meditation audio tape
just in case he wants to rethink
that tycoon script.

Size Six

I hate my body, she said
pretending to eschew
the tiny dessert before her.
She warned me I would gain weight
at our stylish retirement village.

I doubted her advice
added salt to the overcooked veal
and thought about the thin and the rich.
Was she serious? Is thin somehow better?
Was she fishing for a fashion complement?

When I joked about my portly father
and my size 12 love of pasta
her face fell into her undressed salad
as I made a mental dietary note
to order surf and turf the next time.

Camera Shy

With her coffee cup in hand
she immediately sat down and asked
whether I had seen the cameras
upstairs on the church pillars.
I said I hadn't.

She sipped coffee and persisted.
They were everywhere, she said.
To calm her fears, I ventured that
they were just recording the service.
She believed otherwise.

Deciding to shift toward compliance,
I told her my sister drinks coffee
and talks about cameras on her rooftop
The woman hesitated. Then I said,
The CIA really does follow people.
And she got up and left.

Book Garden

Leather or laminated
gold edge or deckle
first edition or last.

Family books have been harvested
from fields of Irish Diaspora,
Plantation Life, Emancipation,
War and The Depression.

Decorative nameplates and proud crests
that have been seeded and weeded
will be lost and found elsewhere
in the family gardens of time.

Ave Maria

At twilight that late fall evening
I absorbed the reality
of your fatherly advice.
You said I might remain alone
as did my widowed grandmother.

I looked at your veined and freckled hands,
your hair made white by early loss,
the fairytale romance with my mother
whose career and children confounded
the promising family legacy.

For years, we watched and waited
each in our own way.

Sipping coffee by the living room window
she remained angry about the life
she never had. Before dinner
she spoke wistfully about college, but
between rages she was left to drift.

The house would rumble and then go silent
as we ignored her inarticulate dreams
as well as her depression.
We managed to survive.
Some of us were better, others worse.

Your final request honors our painful vigil
as I plant two yews by Mary on the Cross
in a peaceful place
of lost dreams and found reality.

Menu Choices

I smoothed the tablecloth wrinkles
as my old linen jacket said,
Say the right things and decide
who should sit where
at this music school luncheon.

Three vases of small pink roses
were provided by a flower committee
to which I did not belong.
And yet, we were equally grateful
for the support of community leaders.

My table seating worked its magic
as we discussed student talent and
management issues often neglected
by music-loving trustees who want
simple solutions to complex lives.

After some discrete petits fours
thankful donors exited the room,
until a wiry widow stopped to mention
her late husband's lofty credentials
and her lovely home in Florida.

As I thought about marrying well
and calling the caterer (instead of
planning donor luncheons)
I winced at the thought of career detours
in support of worthy causes.

Should I suggest we eat light
and let those sweet memories
gently rise to the top?

HOPES & DREAMS

"We dance for laughter, we dance for tears,
we dance for madness, we dance for fears,
we dance for hopes, we dance for screams,
we are the dancers, we create the dreams."

Albert Einstein

Parallel Lives

Long ago peasant dresses
used to be made
from worn-out curtains.
That saved money and some pride.

I set aside the scissors,
the needle and the thread
and watch the hallway curtains
in the open-window breeze.

Teasing the gauze in and out
they dance like white, waltzing wings
that have been set to distant music
that sounds like a harpsichord.

Perhaps it is Marie Antoinette,
I muse, whose naïve cotton whim
would be oblivious to slaves
toiling another continent away.

Full Circle

Our shared studio
and quirky storefront
began our unlikely journeys

as our dreams shifted
through marriage, career
and our now fading hair.

Your science illustrations
and my educational fundraising
ran their sensible courses.

We now pen words
pull city yard weeds and
sketch local pond scenery.

Children, grandchildren and the
living spaces that we own
now own us.

Their clutter and comfort tell us
we've done as good a job
as any suburban housewife

with a handyman and lawn guy
to fantasize about
in that other zip code of life.

The Power of Paint

The paint store window
in this trendy southern town
displays a little orange machine,
which catches her patio-moss eye.

"Can I rent the power washer?"
she asks the clerk in his Harley shirt.
"It's a paint sprayer, and we don't rent."
"So, I can't buy it, either?" she quips.

Standing in the stockroom shadows
a dark-skinned teen smiles at this VW muse
and her plucky, white-haired interest
in paint and power washing.

The Building Committee

Eight gleaming shovels
are lined up in precise verticals
against a carefully draped platform.
Polished bronze doors, still closed,
frame the worthy participants
attending this groundbreaking ceremony.

The Chairman of the Board
stretches his suburban-fit arms
to thank one and all for their generosity.
The Community Spokesperson
in a dark suit, white shirt and a red-striped tie
stands tall and clears his throat.

Seated at the end of this select row
the Minister adjusts his angel-motif tie
and mentally composes his blessing
as the Museum Director
reviews his speech about fine art.

He squints in the late-day sun but
with a job offer on his desk
and stylish housing secured elsewhere,
he knows another building-expansion project
awaits his fundraising skills.

At the center of it all
the Asian eyes of the rising-star architect
float above budgets and politics
as he tilts his head and marvels
at his most unlikely journey from Taiwan.

Golf Queries A–Z

Is the Alligator by the pond
or by the Bunker near the green?
Shall I ask the Caddy by the shack
about the Divot I forgot to put back
or the Eagle in the tree who sees it all?

A Fresh Glove's in my pocket
and a Hot Dog's in my hand.
I'm ready but then wonder.

Is this game an Illusion
or just the Joke of the day?

What use is Knowledge
when I've lost my League status
and my Morning swing tempo
has gone with the wind?

(After-game Nachos like to agree
Optimists with Pars
can play Sundays for free.)

Ahead of the rain
I'll just Quit the front nine
then wave at the young Ranger
Twirl my Umbrella, tip my Visor
And click my Waterproof shoes.

My X-ray ball finder shows
a Yellow clubhouse ahead
so I'll Zip up my golf bag
and called it a day.

Farm Song Lyrics

Let it be, the creek water whispers
in this grove of waning ash trees
where cattle have wallowed
in the summer heat.

Their legs sink into the mud
as they rise up with soulful eyes
begging for respite from the flies
and their fate just down the road.

In the farm's cool shade,
sleek mares nurse their foals.
Their horseshoes are custom made
while the bluegrass works its magic.

After seventy years of ups and downs
the farm is now self-sufficient.
Something I'm proud of,
And yet...

I question its future.
A family of starlings seems to answer
as they escape down the chimney
of our shared legacy farmhouse.

In the hush of evening gratitude
silent barns and mended fences murmur
This land is your land,
This land is mine.

Museum Stroll

Escaping the internet bustle
of my well-informed city
I switched off my cell phone
and retreated to a Paris suburb.

One lily pad has been placed
upper right, two lower left
three more, bottom center.
I stop counting.

Monet's broken brushstrokes
"appeal to generations of art lovers."
Some also say Impressionist wallpaper
will go with living room décor.

What about the world's other *isms*?
Expressionism and Romanticism?
Has the Realism of the camera
finally showed the world too much?

The Curator thinks it has
and rehangs the pond paintings
to sooth urban angst
lily pad by lily pad.

Self-Esteem

They sit motionless in their mascara fog
until the music calls them to the dance floor
and their partners lead intricate steps
they have practiced to distraction.

Looking at their slim partners they
flourish bejeweled arms and wrists.
Their slim legs and glued hair
hide imperfections behind perfection.

Are they shy?
Then why the tight clothes?
Modest?
Then why the rhinestones and cleavage?

They look past me as I return from the dance floor
brimming with pride in my bling-less blue dress
low-heeled shoes and little dangly earrings.
Sometimes, I wink: "Less is More."

Crazy Mood

Some may adore
Armani's latest creation
so elegant, in fact, ecstatic
but give me some nectar from Costco
where the pompous don't argue
about bargain-priced deli meats.

Aisles of beehive shoppers
bewitched by sale prices
gesture toward free nibbles on a tray
while still others mumble prosaic
slightly weird tongue twisters which
a bumblebee would just ignore.

Three-Four Time

She stops mid-spin
in a blur of a silk watercolors
making a fast-reverse turn
reaching out to the adoring crowds
eager for their approval.

When her partner pulls her back
along their waltzing line
they race counterclockwise before
the row of worthy judges with
official scoreboard checklists.

The music continues
while the next hopeful couple
comes into focus, turning
this way and that to eagerly claim
their Moment of Fame.

Duffers

This cloudy morning
a ray of sunshine
moves across the short grass,
and The Dimpled Ball
slowly roles over the lip,
into the bunker
silently wondering why
these retired gents
can't swing easy
instead of slicing and hooking,
trying to prove they still
have what it takes.

Tango Moments

Her shoes move first, then her hips.
Her weighted skirt picks up speed
winding and unwinding around her legs
just as the costume maker planned.
Then the shoulders do their work.
Artful arms slowly extend
each hand to their jeweled fingers.

Suddenly, they all pause with the music.
Some reach for each other
while others stay apart
shifting weight, turning a head
or preparing for a fast run
to outpace the couples behind.

Who knows what's next
in this rhythmic blur of bejeweled bling?

The dinner guests, many of whom
are dancers themselves,
forget to eat. They are dazzled
by the music and the plastic trophies.

The dancers are determined
to catch the judges' eyes

as slim young men partner
swirling divas (some of whom
are twice their age). Together
they seek fame or just a little nostalgia
in the magic of their timeless tangos.

Pieces of Cotton

Appliqué is a fancy word for Apply.

After my scissors had made
their simple sunset shapes,
pieces of fabric were put
wherever my straight pins pleased.

Reds or blues, morning or evening
my patches of color became pictures
of roads taken and not taken.
Choices over choices.

When a friend said follow your dream
I bought needles and threads
then applied for craft fair booths
during those Hopeful Hippie Years
of all-natural cotton.

Shipboard Romance

How easily I flew home and
put an ocean between us.

(Bird-watching at both land and sea
was our shared dream,
binoculars held steady
as we searched for puffins and pilot whales.)

Leaning into the heavy door I knew so well
I found things at home unchanged:
the faint mustiness of
my grandmother's blue rug and
some Earl Grey tea.

I opened my mail,
called a few friends,
sat in her settee
And then . . .
I began to miss you.

Could I have understood too well
your wistful poetry
and too easily retrieved my floating heart
from an ocean of possibilities?

To stay safe in my Boston harbor
listening from afar for the mailman
then looking at maps and flight schedules
letting paper plans and projects fill the void?

Should I have let your shipboard verses
pilot me toward an unlikely shore
or quietly retreat and let your memory
simply float out to sea?

Suburban Myth

Once there was sky.
And there were orange blossoms.
But now . . .
the heavens cast a magical glow
on torn petals floating in a cloudy pool
he had never seen before.

Always searching for self,
Narcissus gazes down
trying to remember why
he left the safety of his suburban town
and returned to this forbidden lake.

In autumn they had argued
and left in anger.
Their words had Echoed across the water.
And he feared that the lake and the dinner
had cast a spell on him
tarnishing his beauty as she ladled
the duck sauce onto his plate.
He suspected she used powerful herbs
from this mossy bank to question,
interrogate and then destroy his
senior prom image for her own purposes.

But why did she do all this, he wondered?
To be more beautiful, herself?
Or just take home a shiny trophy
to impress her suburban parents?

Stay-at-Home Dad

Tethered to his leash and his cell phone,
a young dad seeks city park relief from
the baby carriage and his wife's poodle.

The grass at his feet has been worn bare
by parents and grandparents who smile
at the sounds of an ice-cream truck.

Assured that his little son is still sleeping
the stay-at-home dad texts his friends
and studies a few more parenting skills online.

Patience

Picture a pitcher of
lemonade on a hot day!

Patterns of sweat
trickling down the glass
onto a soft green tablecloth.

A star-like pattern
of lemon-slice pulp
peers through the glass
like a noontime starburst.
Then sugar begins falling to the bottom,
as three lemons patiently await their turn.

Milton Keynes UK
Ingram Content Group UK Ltd.
UKHW050807201123
432900UK00011B/295

9 798822 917538